It's Cloudy Today

Kristin Sterling

Lerner Publications Company

Minneapolis

Dedicated to
cloud watchers
of all ages

Lerner Publications Company
A division of Lerner Publishing Group, Inc.
241 First Avenue North
Minneapolis, MN 55401 U.S.A.

Website address: www.lernerbooks.com

Library of Congress Cataloging-in-Publication Data

Sterling, Kristin.
    It's Cloudy today / by Kristin Sterling.
        p.   cm. — (Lightning Bolt Books™—What's the weather like?)
    Includes index.
    978-0-7613-4256-4 (lib. bdg. : alk. paper)
    1. Clouds—Juvenile literature.
  QC921.35.S74 2010
    551.57'6—dc22   2008051585

Manufactured in the United States of America
1 2 3 4 5 6 — BP — 15 14 13 12 11 10

Contents

Cloud Watcher — page 4

What Are Clouds? — page 14

Cloudy Day Fun — page 20

Another Cloudy Day — page 26

Activity — page 28

Did You Know? — page 29

Glossary — page 30

Further Reading — page 31

Index — page 32

Cloud Watcher

Lie on your back and look up at the sky. It's a perfect cloudy day.

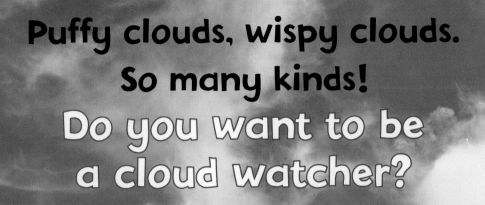

Puffy clouds, wispy clouds.
So many kinds!
Do you want to be
a cloud watcher?

You can watch for clouds as soft and wispy as bird feathers.

These are called cirrus clouds.

Cirrus clouds form high in the sky—about 30,000 feet (9,144 meters) above Earth.

They tell us good weather is on the way.

You can watch for clouds as white and puffy as cotton balls.

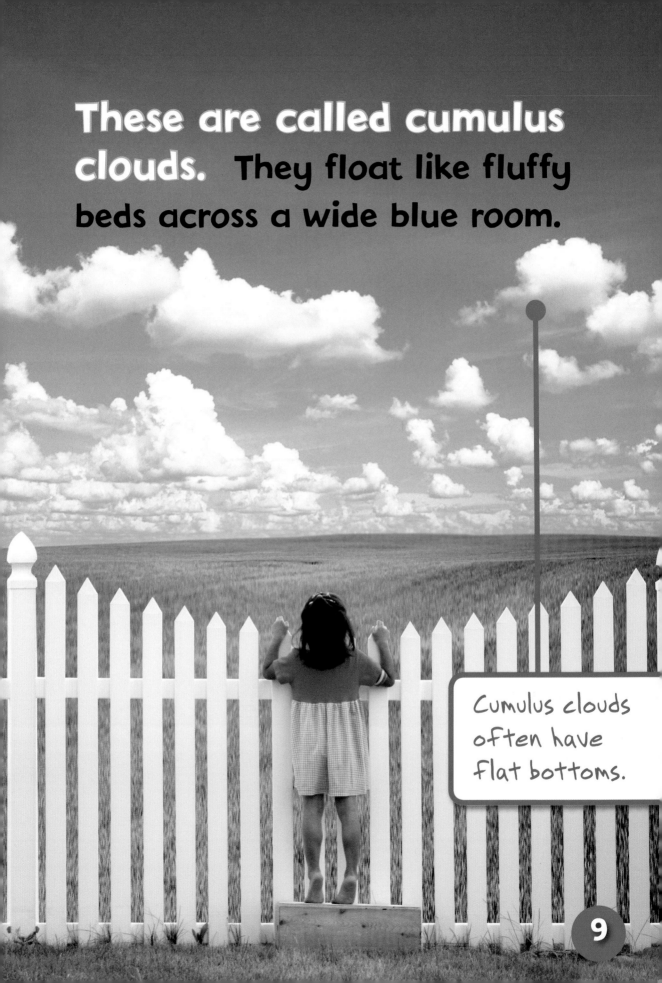

These are called cumulus clouds. They float like fluffy beds across a wide blue room.

Cumulus clouds often have flat bottoms.

You can watch for clouds as flat and gray as dusty books.

These are called stratus clouds.

Stratus clouds bring dark, gray weather.

They hang low in the sky, waiting to spill rain.

You can watch for clouds
that touch the ground.

This is called fog.

Fog is produced
when air is
warmer than land.

What Are Clouds?

Clouds are collections of tiny water droplets or ice crystals.

Ice is often an ingredient in clouds.

14

Raindrops and snowflakes fall from clouds.

Rain is falling from these clouds.

Clouds are pushed in every direction by the wind.

Some clouds move quickly and some move slowly.

Clouds speed across the sky above New York City.

Meteorologists are people who study weather patterns.

Meteorologists get information about clouds.

They use many kinds of tools to predict the weather.

Cloudy Day Fun

What can you do on a cloudy day?

You can imagine that the sky is filled with cloud stories.

Cloud watching is fun when you use your imagination.

There is a big white bird swooping to Earth. Do you see its pointy beak and round, fluffy belly?

People see many different things in clouds. What does this cloud look like to you?

This is a dog running through the sky.

You can fly
through a cloud
in an airplane.

Now you are higher
than the clouds!

Another Cloudy Day

The wind sweeps the clouds away. Another cloudy day has ended.

What will you do on the next cloudy day?

Activity
You Can Make Clouds

Ask an adult if you can make shaving cream clouds. To make your clouds, you'll need a plastic tablecloth and a can of shaving cream.

First, cover a table with the tablecloth. Then, pretend the table is a sky filled with clouds. Use the shaving cream to make thin, feathery cirrus clouds near the top of the sky. Make fat, puffy cumulus clouds in the middle of the sky. Create long, flat stratus clouds across the bottom of the sky. Now you have a sky filled with clouds!

When it's time to clean up, wipe the tablecloth off with a wet towel.

Did You Know?

Luke Howard was a chemist and businessman who lived in England. He loved watching clouds. He named the clouds using Latin words: cirrus, cumulus, nimbus, and stratus. These are names that scientists continue to use.

Cirrus means curl of hair.

Cumulus is a Latin word meaning heap.

Stratus means layer.

Nimbus is a Latin word meaning rain.

Glossary

cirrus cloud: an icy, wispy cloud that forms high in the sky

cloud: a mass of water droplets or ice crystals floating in the air

cumulus cloud: a white, puffy cloud

fog: a cloud that forms close to the ground

meteorologist: a person who studies weather patterns

stratus cloud: a flat, gray cloud that hangs low in the sky

Further Reading

Hannah, Julie, and Joan Holub. *The Man Who Named the Clouds*. Morton Grove, IL: Albert Whitman & Company, 2006.

Locker, Thomas. *Cloud Dance*. San Diego: Harcourt, 2000.

Shaw, Charles G. *It Looked Like Spilt Milk*. New York: Harper Trophy, 1988.

Weather Dude
http://www.wxdude.com

Weather Wiz Kids
http://www.weatherwizkids.com

Web Weather for Kids
http://eo.ucar.edu/webweather

Index

activity, 28

cirrus clouds, 6–7, 29
cumulus clouds, 8–9, 29

fog, 12–13

Howard, Luke, 29

ice crystals, 14

meteorologists, 18–19

nimbus clouds, 29

rain, 11, 15

snow, 15
stratus clouds, 10–11, 29

wind, 16, 26

Photo Acknowledgments

The images in this book are used with the permission of: © ULTRA F.©Photodisc/Getty Images, p. 1; © Agg/Dreamstime.com, p. 2; © Flamingo Photography/Gallo Images ROOTS RF Collection/Getty Images, p. 4; © Roine Magnussen/Digital Vision/Getty Images, p. 5; © Mcech/Dreamstime.com, p. 6; Courtesy of NOAA /Captain Albert E. Theberge Jr., NOAA Corps, p. 7; © Marta Johnson, p. 8; © age fotostock/SuperStock, p. 9; © Photodisc/Getty Images, p. 10; © Searagen/Dreamstime.com, p. 11; © Thierry Bouzac/Impact/The Image Works, p. 12; © Jarek78/Dreamstime.com, p. 13; © Kate Powers/Taxi/Getty Images, p. 14; © Creatista/Dreamstime.com, p. 15; © John Grant/Stone/Getty Images, p. 16; © Anton Prado/snapvillage, p. 17; © Joe Readle/Getty Images, p. 18; © J. Baylor Roberts/National Geographics/Getty Images, p. 19; © Toni Johnson/snapvillage, p. 20; © iStockphoto.com/JaquelineSouthby, p. 21; © Corbis/SuperStock, p. 22; © age fotostock/SuperStock, p. 23; © Reflexstock/First Light/Paul Austring, p. 24; © flashon/snapvillage, p. 25; © Christopher Thomas/Getty Images, p. 26; © janenwicklund/snapvillage.com, p. 27; © Todd Strand/Independent Picture Service, p. 28; © SSPL/The Image Works, p. 29; © Stuart Redler/Taxi/Getty Images, p. 30; © Kohel Hara/Taxi Japan/Getty Images, p. 31.

Front Cover: istockphoto.com/Derek Dammann.